Quickie Handles a Loss

By Donald Driver

Illustrated by Joe Groshek

© 2009 Donald J. Driver

ISBN: 978-0-615-32984-0

Printed in the US by Worzalla. First printing November 2009

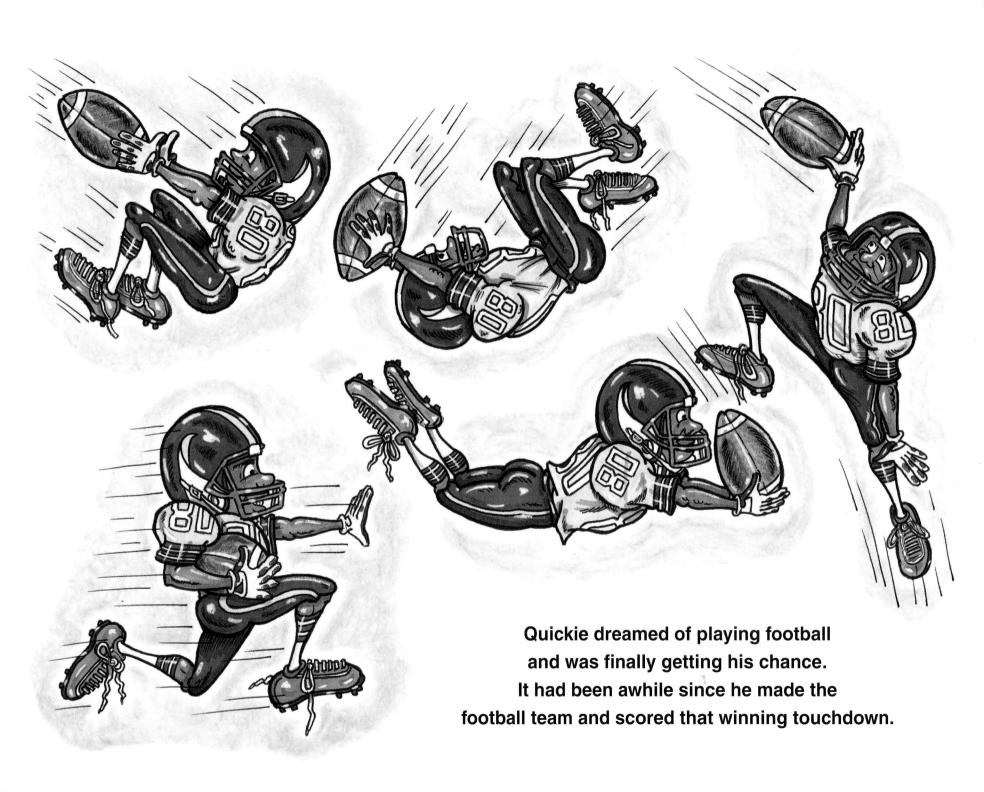

Quickie dreamed of playing football
and was finally getting his chance.
It had been awhile since he made the
football team and scored that winning touchdown.

The team has been giving it their all
and had not lost a game.
The football season was going great.
Quickie and his teammates were unstoppable!

The playoffs were
weeks away,
and the boys practiced
even harder and longer.

One day, during the walk home from practice, Quickie passed his neighbor's house and noticed a litter of puppies inside a box. He quickly went over to take a closer look.

"These puppies are so cute!" Quickie shouted.
"Mr. Peters, may I take one home, please?"
Mr. Peters explained to Quickie that he
must ask his parents first.

Quickie ran home
as fast as he could.
He found his mom and dad
outside working in the yard,
and his little sister Christina
playing with her toys.

Excited and out of breath, Quickie yelled,
"May I have a puppy?"
With a look of surprise, his father asked,
"Son, what did you say?"
"A puppy! May I have a puppy from Mr. Peter's
house? May I please have one?" Quickie pleaded.

"Oh honey, that's a big responsibility," Quickie's mom said.
"Mom, I'll help Quickie take good care of it,"
Christina said excitedly.
Please? Please, may we have a puppy?"

Dad slowly replied, "We'll think about it."
Quickie and Christina jumped for joy at the thought of having their very own puppy.

"The next day at school,
Quickie met his best friend
Bill out front like always,
but Bill looked very upset.
"What's wrong?" Quickie asked.

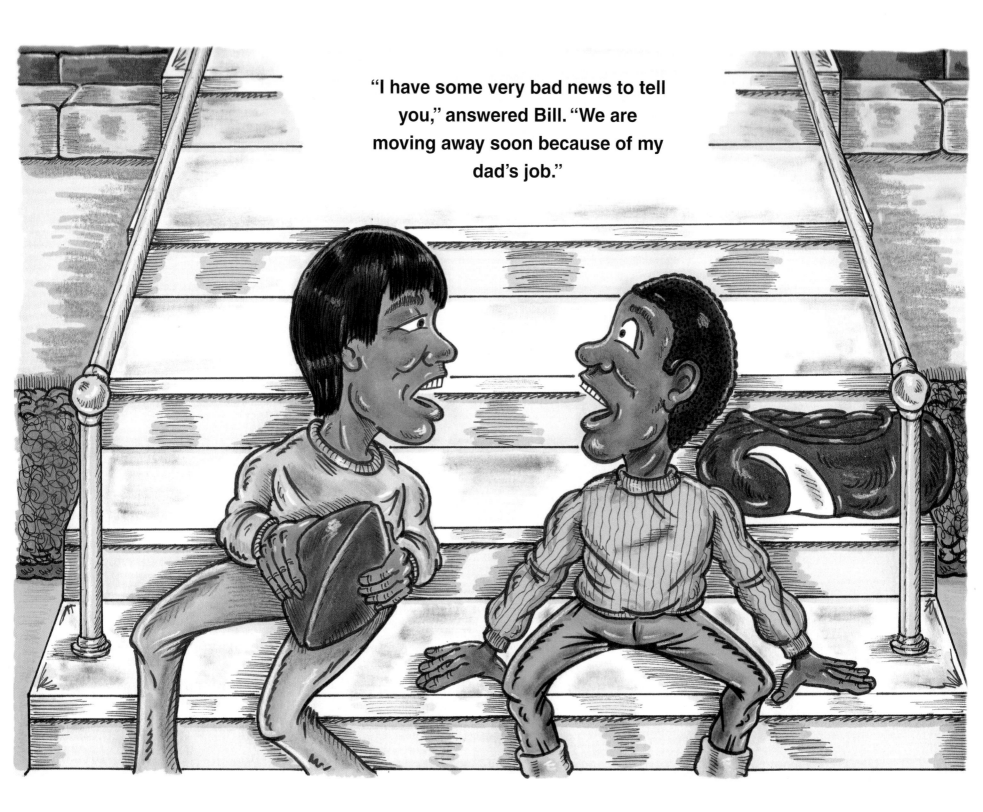

The thought of losing his best friend
was heavy on his mind.
After school, Quickie told
his parents about the sad news.

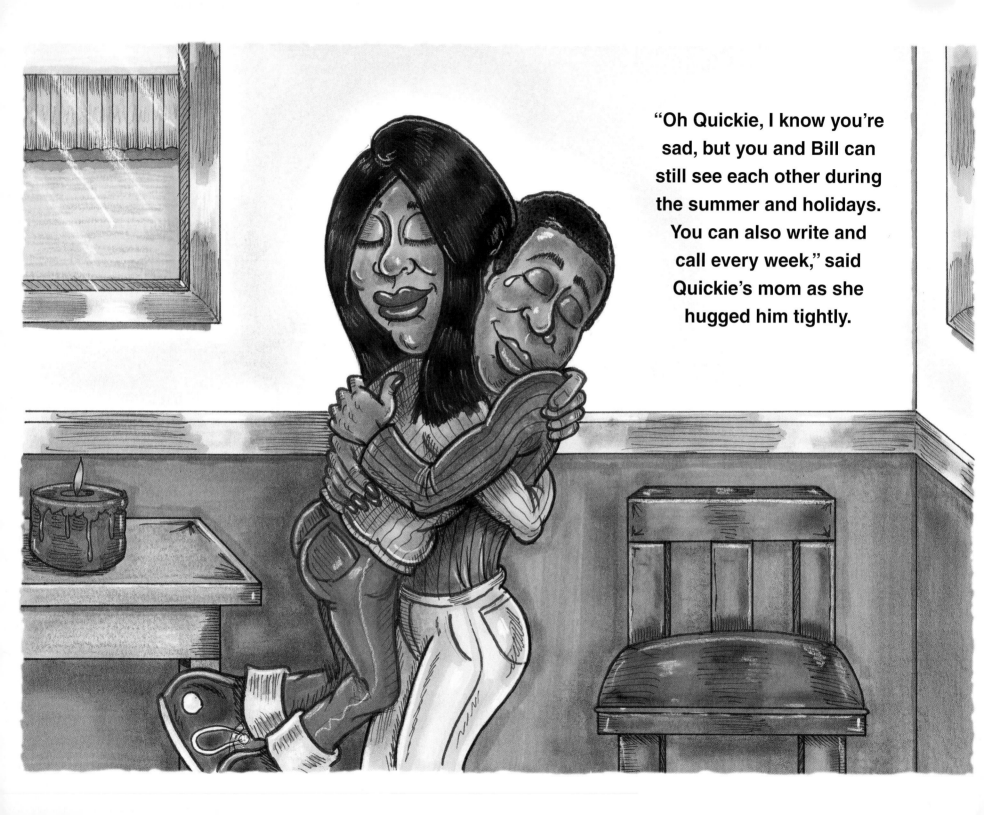

"Oh Quickie, I know you're sad, but you and Bill can still see each other during the summer and holidays. You can also write and call every week," said Quickie's mom as she hugged him tightly.

Soon Quickie started to feel better and said,
"I guess you are right Mom. Bill and I will always
be best friends no matter how far apart we are."

As the week continued, Bill and Quickie spent more time together laughing and getting ready for the playoff game. They knew Bill would be leaving soon and they agreed not to spend their last days together being sad.

Bill reached deep into a pile of toys, pulled out a football with the team colors, and handed it to Quickie. "It's my favorite, and I want my best friend to have it." said Bill. "Wow, thanks Bill! I promise to take good care of it," said Quickie.

As the days went by, Bill's family decided to leave sooner than they had planned. Bill was very upset he was leaving early and would not be able to play in the playoff game. On that afternoon, his parents took him to visit Quickie to say goodbye before leaving.

Bill slowly walked up to ring the doorbell and Quickie answered the door. "Hi Bill, what are you doing here?" Sadly, Bill answered, "I just wanted to come over to say goodbye. My parents and I are leaving tomorrow morning and I will not be able to play in the game next week." The two best friends gave each other one final hug before saying goodbye.

The next day Quickie watched until their truck was out of his sight. He ran inside, went straight to his room, and threw himself onto the bed. Dad and Christina came into the room and tried to cheer him up. "Just because Bill and his family moved away doesn't mean you will lose your best friend," said Quickie's dad.

It was almost time for the playoff game. Quickie and the team really missed Bill, but they still practiced hard. Just before Quickie left to go to the ballpark on game day, he received a call from Bill wishing the team good luck. Receiving that call made Quickie very happy and he raced out the door.

During the game, the team played very hard. Still they were trailing behind by seven points with only two minutes to go. Despite their best efforts, the opposing team won the game. Quickie and his teammates walked off the field with their heads hung low.

Once in the locker room, their coach told them all how proud he was. "You all did your best out there, and I am very proud to be your coach. Sometimes you'll win and sometimes you'll lose, but the important thing is to always do your very best each time you step out on the field," said Coach Marvin.

On the ride home, Quickie sat quietly in the back seat. His parents and little sister tried to cheer him up, but still Quickie sat quietly looking out the window.

Once inside the house, he ran straight to his room again. This time he noticed a box on the floor and walked over to it. What a surprise he found inside that box. "A puppy, a puppy!" Quickie shouted with a huge smile on his face. He picked up the little brown bundle of happiness.

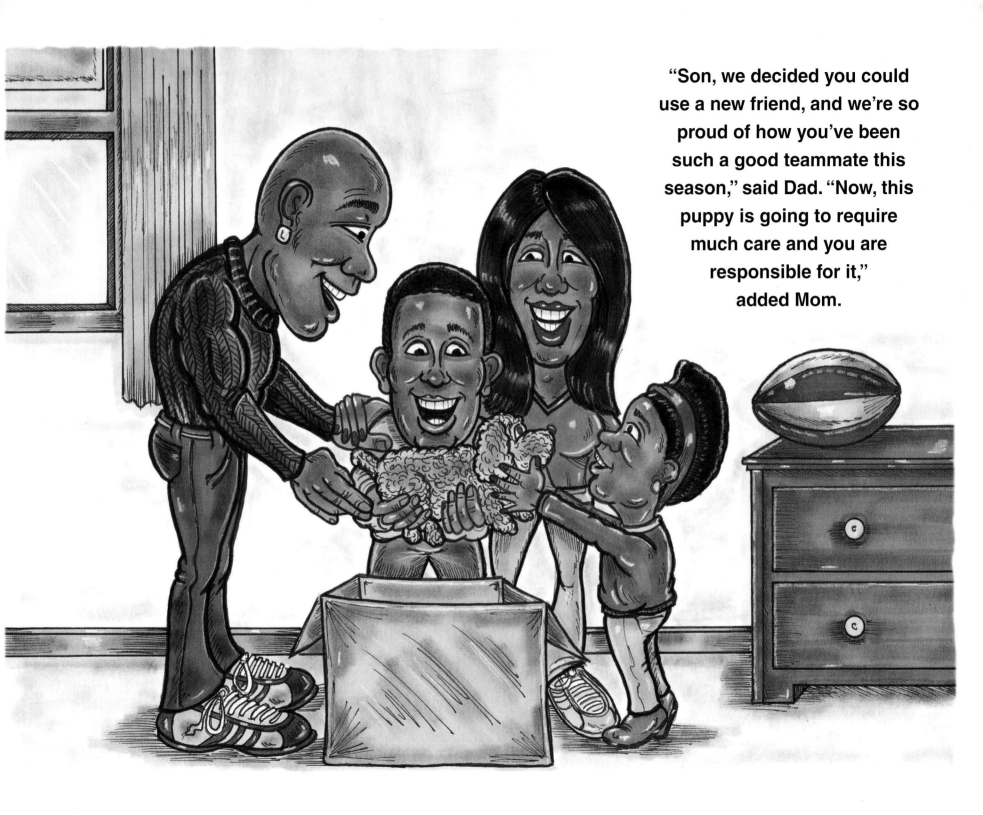

"Son, we decided you could use a new friend, and we're so proud of how you've been such a good teammate this season," said Dad. "Now, this puppy is going to require much care and you are responsible for it," added Mom.

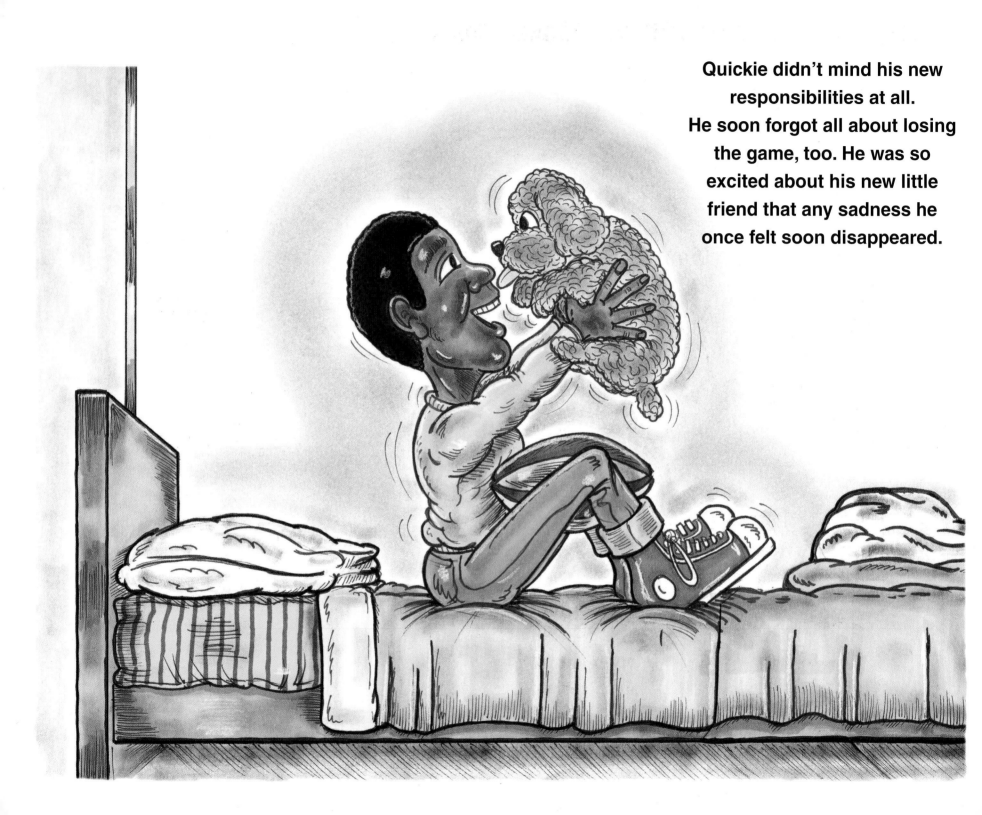

Quickie didn't mind his new responsibilities at all. He soon forgot all about losing the game, too. He was so excited about his new little friend that any sadness he once felt soon disappeared.